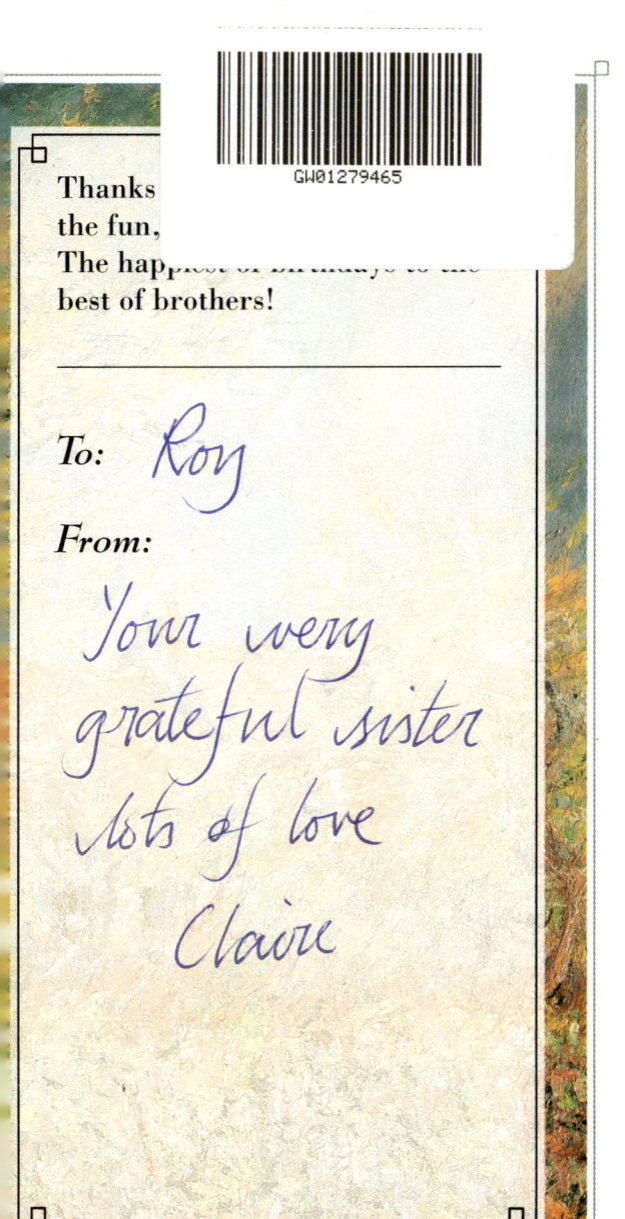

Thanks ... for all
the fun, ...
The happiest of birthdays to the
best of brothers!

To: Roy

From:

Your very
grateful sister
lots of love
Claire

May the coming year bring
you encouragement and
praise, times of adventure,
times of contentment.
Friendship, love.
And a little bit of luck.
May it be one that you'll
look back on with a sigh
of satisfaction – a year
of marvels.

Brothers teach you a lot.
Soccer, swimming, how to
skip pebbles, to skateboard, to
climb tall trees.
But mostly – how to be friends.
How to survive arguments.
How to share. How to forgive.
How to be human.

We've come a long way together.
You know who I really am
and what made me so.
There's never any need for show
or lame excuses.
We accept and love each other,
faults and all.

Everyone needs a brother
just like you.
To thump and hug.
To quarrel with
and make up with.
To share adventures
and secrets.
And to love.

However important you are, however respected and respectable, however distinguished, however wise – I know about Father Bear and the humming top and the moth-eaten rabbit in the attic. And smile – and love you all the better.
You are forever my dear, kind, loving brother wearing a disguise.

There would be times
you took the blame.
And times
I did the same for you.
We are a team,
we two.
As Dad said –
"Double Trouble."

Brothers know all their siblings' deepest, darkest secrets.
All the terrible *faux pas*.
All the failures.
All the disasters.
All the stupidities.
And keep their mouths shut.
(Thanks!)

To the world we may be capable, efficient – even sophisticated. But you and I remember mud and bonfires, the solemn burial of mice, dressing up and sword fights. Shared secrets. Shared terrors. Shared laughter. I raise my glass to you.... The real you. The real me.

Some brothers can mend fuses and clear drains and paint ceilings and take cuttings and find out why the car won't go. Some brothers have other gifts. You've always been there when I needed you. You help to hold my <u>life</u> together.

With a tack or two, a piece of string, a dab of glue, and a kind arm round my shoulders.

—◇—

Thank you for all the times you've rescued me and comforted me. And fought my battles. What would I do without you?

When one is very very small the best defence is always the same.
"I'll tell my bruvver of you."
The cry goes back to the cave.
The ultimate deterrent.
Thank you for all the times you rescued me.
Or got thumped, trying.

Such a big world and everything to learn. So many strangers. So many choices. How good to know you're there – my first companion and first friend. With you I can relax and smile, knowing you understand, and accept me as I am.

Thank you for always being there for me – however many the miles between us. Your voice on the phone, your writing on an envelope, your special knock, your grin, the sure clasp of your hand – mean it is all going to come right.